Written by Deborah Murrell and Liz Scoggins

Illustrated by Kelly Waldek and Trevor Dunton

Edited by Ellen Bailey and Rachel Carter

Designed by Angie Allison and Zoe Quayle

Produced by Joanne Rooke

Picture Acknowledgments

Corbis: Front cover and title page
ShutterStock Inc.: Back cover

ShutterStock Inc.: pages 6–7, 8–9, 11, 12–13, 14–15, 18 (except dolphin and ostrich), 19, 20–21, 25, 26–27, 28–29, 30–31, 38–39, 40–41, 42–43 (except blue whale and wolf), 44–45 (except sloth, blue whale, cicada, kittiwake, skunk, stick insect, wolverine, tiger shark, mosquito), 46 (orangutan), 48, 50–51, 52–53, 54–55, 58–59 (except penguin, hedgehog, rhino, orangutan and elephant). iStockphoto: pages 18 (dolphin and ostrich), 43 (wolf), 44–45 (sloth, blue whale, cicada, kittiwake, skunk, stick insect, wolverine, tiger shark, mosquito), 46 (macaque), 58–59 (penguin, hedgehog, rhino, orangutan and elephant). SuperStock Inc.: 42 and 44 (blue whale).

The publisher and authors disclaim as far as is legally permissible all liability for accidents or injuries or loss that may occur as a result of information or instructions given in this book. Use your best common sense at all times: always wear appropriate safety gear, be very careful with scissors, stay within the law and local rules, and be considerate of other people.

First published in Great Britain in 2007 by Buster Books,
an imprint of Michael O'Mara Books Limited,
9 Lion Yard, Tremadoc Road,
London SW4 7NQ

Copyright © 2007 Buster Books

A CIP catalogue record for this book is available from the British Library.

978-1-906082-05-5

2 4 6 8 10 9 7 5 3 1

Printed and bound in Italy by L.E.G.O.

Papers used by Buster Books are natural, recyclable products made from wood grown in sustainable forests. The manufacturing processes conform to the environmental regulations of the country of origin.

I Love
Animals
Annual 2008

Buster Books

CONTENTS

INTRODUCTION

If you are mad about monkeys, crazy for crocodiles, or loopy about lions, then look no further. You'll go totally wild for the animals in this book.

Packed with fun facts, this is the perfect place to read up on your favourite wild animals. The tallest, fastest, smallest and largest are right here. This book will take you all around the world in search of the creatures you love.

There are quizzes and games to keep you on your toes, plus puzzles, paper crafts and great ideas for projects you can try at home. You'll never be at a loose end again.

Learn why some animals are in serious danger and how you can help. Find out the exciting things animals get up to, and choose the perfect animal to adopt.

Discover how to make best friends with a horse, what keeps a zebra hidden and how to handle a rampaging rhino.

Soon you'll be able to impress everyone with all the cool things you know about animals — whether it's the average size of a giraffe, or how to track animals in the wild.

From cute cubs to confident kings of the jungle, lions are the only cats that live in groups called 'prides'.

WHAT KIND OF ANIMAL ARE YOU?

If you were an animal, what kind of animal would you be? You can find out what your answers mean on page 60, but don't be a cheetah!

1. How do you behave at school?

A. I concentrate well and remember everything easily.

B. I get lonely if my friends aren't about.

C. I work hard and always pay attention in class.

D. I get distracted in the classroom.

E. I look forward to break time so I can go out and play.

2. If you could have any one of these animals as a pet, which would it be?

A. Something big like a dog, so I won't accidentally squash it.

B. A rabbit, definitely a rabbit.

C. A cute mouse

D. A guinea pig – its little squeaks would make me giggle.

E. A brightly coloured budgie.

3. At the weekend, which would you prefer to do?

A. Make a splash in my local pool.

B. Run around the park with my friends.

C. Visit the local library to get some more books.

D. Play lots of games until Monday morning comes around.

E. Just kick-back and relaaaax.

4. On sports day, which would you rather do?

A. Laze in the sun and watch.

B. Run in every single race.

C. Spend the afternoon writing a story for my friends.

D. Do the egg and spoon race – it's the best!

E. Run one race, but make sure I win it.

5. At school, someone copies your homework. What do you do?

A. Sit on them until they promise not to do it again.

B. Let them copy it.

C. Tell the teacher.

D. Let them copy, but give them the wrong answers.

E. Shout!

6. Which of these would make the perfect snack for you?

A. Peanuts.

B. Mmm, a chicken sandwich.

C. Chocolate mice.

D. Anything.

E. A beefburger.

7. A new kid at school asks to be your friend. What do you do?

A. Let them hang out with me and my friends.

B. Watch them carefully until they prove they'll make a good friend.

C. Spend some time chatting with them before I decide.

D. Welcome them with open arms — the more the merrier.

E. Ignore them completely. I'm too busy to make friends.

8. If you were going to play a game which of these would it be?

A. Memory Mayhem (see page 26).

B. Catch — I never fail to catch the ball.

C. Snakes and Ladders — it's the only game worth playing.

D. Hide and Seek — I'm sure I can win.

E. Chase — I'm the fastest.

WILD ABOUT PETS

Your pet might seem to be the sweetest, fluffiest creature in the world, but don't forget that all pets are the distant relations of wild animals. Once upon a time your adorable puppy's relatives could have hunted in a pack like wolves, and your cute kitten's relatives might have lived on the African plains like lions.

Puppies Get Out And About

Next time you visit the park watch how dogs act around each other.

Most dogs are very friendly and will play together happily. However you might see one hang its tail between its legs and lower its head towards the ground. This is its way of showing respect to another dog. It means that the dog realises the other animal is more powerful and dangerous than itself. A young wolf behaves just like this in front of a more powerful wolf.

Wolves In The Wild

Wolves live together in groups called 'packs'. Packs hunt and play together like one big family. A wolf that isn't in a pack can get very lonely and may howl loudly to attract other wolves.

Pet dogs get lonely, too, if they are left by themselves for a long time, and can howl the house down. They would much rather have someone to play with and can't wait for you to get home each day.

Top Dog

In a pack there is always one wolf in charge. This wolf is usually older than the other wolves and has a strong character that they can look up to.

Dogs need someone to look up to as well and they see their owner as their leader. Don't let your pet think it's top dog!

Puppies love to be in a pack. If you bring a pet puppy home it will miss its brothers and sisters.

Cool Cats

Cats are much more independent than dogs. Except for lions, most of the big cats in the wild prefer to live by themselves. You can easily leave a cat at home alone all day, but you might have to work hard to form a friendship with it.

Cats In Training

If you or a friend has a pet cat why not make up a game to play with it? Soon, you'll be the best of pals.

A simple toy like a piece of string can keep a cat distracted for hours. You'll see the cat crouch low, keep very still, then pounce suddenly. Next time you see a nature programme on TV, watch closely and see how the big cats hunt — do they use the same tactics as a cat with a piece of string?

Keep Out

In the wild, a tiger might defend an area as big as ten football pitches. Just like a tiger, a pet cat will mark out a big area as its own personal cat kingdom.

Your cat will patrol the borders of its territory, guarding against other cats and even fighting them if they try to take over.

Even though a domestic cat is one hundred times smaller than a tiger, its behaviour is very similar.

Kittens don't mind going solo — just like their distant tiger relations.

Jumping Frog

This frog is an excellent jumper – if you get your friends to make frogs too, you can have a froggy race!

Start with a square piece of paper. Green paper makes a good frog, but you could always colour in the paper yourself if you can't find any.

1. With the coloured side face down, fold the paper in half from side to side, and top to bottom. Then flatten out the sheet.

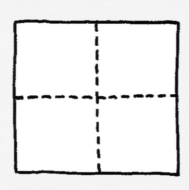

2. Next, fold each corner into the centre to make a smaller square.

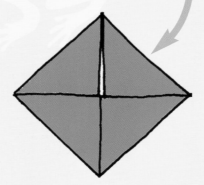

3. Now fold the top left- and top right-hand sides into the middle, making a kite shape.

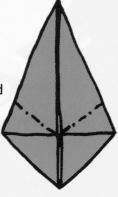

4. Fold up the bottom point of the paper so that you have a triangle, and press it down firmly.

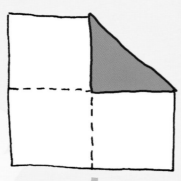

5. Take the bottom two points of your triangle and fold them both into the centre.

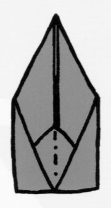

6. Now fold the paper up from the lower edge and press down firmly. Your paper will be getting very thick by now, but don't worry – it will make your frog extra springy!

7. To make the back legs, fold the lower edge back again in a zig-zag.

8. Next, fold the point of the paper over.

9. Lastly, turn your frog over and draw on some eyes.

10. To make the frog jump, press down on its back and flick your finger off. Start racing!

WORLD CHAMPIONS

The world is full of animals that are really amazing. Take a look at this map to see where they come from and why they are so special.

Peregrine falcons live in Scotland, as well as in every other continent apart from Antarctica. They have fantastic eyesight – spotting a tasty snack 5 miles away.

The blue whale is the world's biggest mammal. It can grow to 30 metres long and weigh up to 150 tonnes. Blue whales are warm-blooded animals, so they are called 'mammals', not fish. They live in every ocean.

The grey wolf lives in packs with as many as 20 other wolves. When a young wolf strikes out on its own, it can travel hundreds of kilometres from its family to start a new pack.

The tiniest bird in the world is the bee hummingbird, which comes from Cuba. It only grows to about 5 centimetres in length and can flap its wings an astonishing 80 times a second. That's so fast you can't even see the bird's wings move.

NORTH AMERICA

SOUTH AMERICA

The noisiest animal on land is the howler monkey from South America. The racket it makes sounds like a cross between a donkey braying and a dog barking.

The largest animal on land is the African bush elephant, which grows up to 4 metres tall and can weigh up to 8 tonnes. Elephants charge at a speed of 24 to 40 kilometres per hour when they get angry.

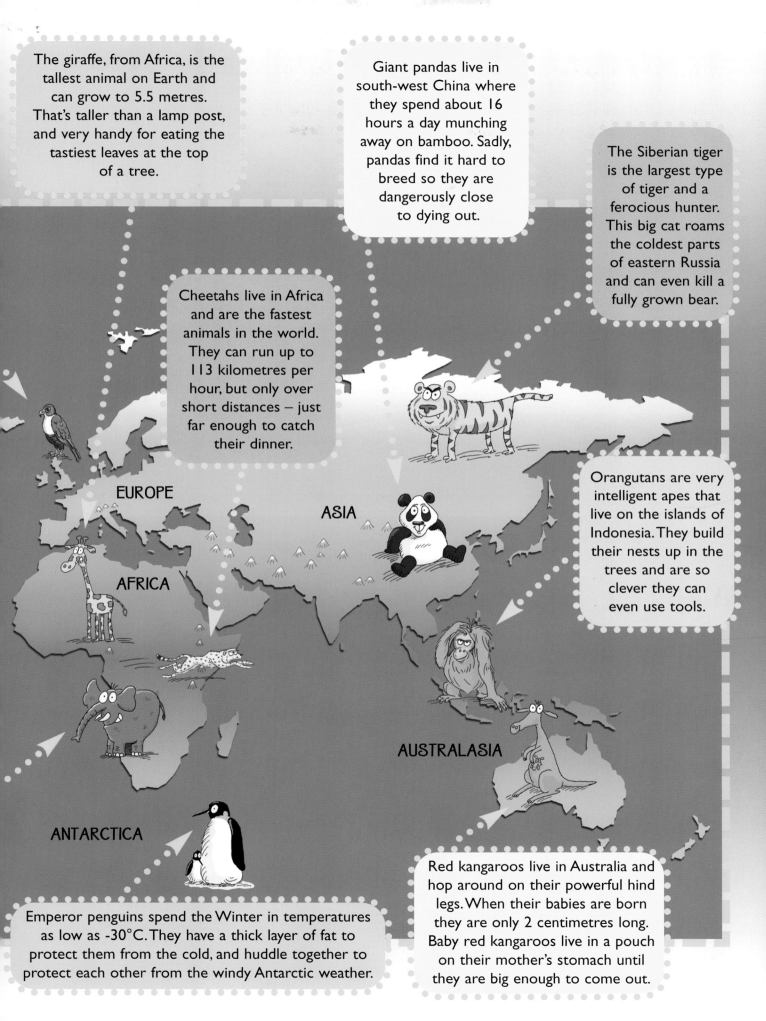

TRUE OR FALSE?

How much do you really know about animals? Decide if the statements below are true or false, then flick to page 60 to see how you've done.

1. All zebras have exactly the same number of stripes.

2. The flamingo is topsy-turvy – it eats with its head upside down.

3. Hummingbirds are the tiniest birds in the whole world.

4. An elephant can run at speeds of over 24 kilometres an hour.

5. Poor hippopotamus – it's the only mammal that can't run.

6. A giraffe's tongue is over 40 centimetres long. Slurp!

7. A butterfly has not one, but two pairs of eyes.

8. A crocodile can't stick out its tongue.

9. Dolphins sleep with both their eyes open.

10. A camel has three eyelids.

11. The brain of an ostrich is as small as its eye.

12. The seahorse is the only animal in the world with a male that gives birth to live babies.

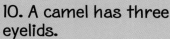

HOW TO TAME A HORSE

Horses and ponies can sometimes be nervous of humans. When approaching a horse or pony there are certain things you can do to help it stay calm. The name 'horse whisperer' is given to a special sort of horse trainer who uses arm movements and eye contact to win the trust of horses. Read the instructions below and put yourself on the path to becoming a horse whisperer.

Softly, Softly

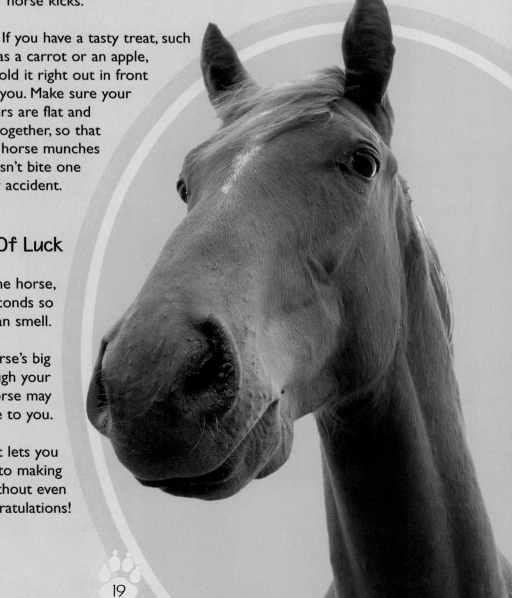

Loose clothing that flaps in the wind can scare our four-legged friends, so wear clothes that fit closely and leave any scarves at home. If you have long hair, tie it back.

Walk up to the horse slowly, but confidently. Horses cannot see straight in front of them, so approach the animal from the left-hand side. Avoid its back legs in case the horse kicks.

If you have a tasty treat, such as a carrot or an apple, hold it right out in front of you. Make sure your fingers are flat and close together, so that when the horse munches the food it doesn't bite one of your fingers by accident.

A Stroke Of Luck

Once you are close to the horse, wait patiently for a few seconds so it gets used to your human smell.

Stand at a safe distance from the horse's big nostrils and breathe out gently through your nose. If you're in luck, the horse may well do the same to you.

Gently stroke the horse's neck. If it lets you do this, you are well on the way to making the animal your best friend without even ruffling its mane. Congratulations!

START A CLUB

A conservation club is a great way to raise awareness of the dangers facing your favourite animal. So what are you waiting for? Round up a group of friends and decide which animal you'd all like to support. It could be anything from the beautiful blue whale, to a creature that lives on your doorstep. Once you've worked out which animal is your favourite, start organising your club.

1. It's All In The Name

Choose a catchy club name like 'The Rhino Rescue Club' or 'The Happy Hedgehog Club'. Then cut out the membership cards from the next page and get everyone to fill in the club's name, their name and the animal you've chosen to support.

2. Your First Club Meeting

You could hold the first meeting at your house. Alternatively, ask your school if you can use a classroom at lunchtime.

You'll need to decide how often to meet, what activities to do, how to raise money for your chosen animal, and most importantly, how to find out more about it. Make sure that everyone in the club gets a fair say when making decisions.

3. Fundraising

Why not raise some money for a charity that helps your favourite animal? You could organise a sponsored silence, and ask friends and family to give you money for every hour you keep silent. Or write to local businesses to ask if they'd be willing to make donations.

4. Activities

Don't forget to have fun! You could organise trips to your local park to spot signs of wildlife activity (see page 36), or ask your school if you can take a trip to a zoo or safari park for a real adventure. How about baking some biscuits in the shape of your club animal?

MEMBERSHIP CARD

The. . . . . .Club
Name:. . . . .
(founding member)
We support:
. . . . in the wild.

MEMBERSHIP CARD

The. . . . . .Club
Name:. . . . .
(founding member)
We support:
. . . . in the wild.

MEMBERSHIP CARD

The. . . . . .Club
Name:. . . . .
(founding member)
We support:
. . . . in the wild.

MEMBERSHIP CARD

The. . . . . .Club
Name:. . . . .
(founding member)
We support:
. . . . in the wild.

MEMBERSHIP CARD

The. . . . . .Club
Name:. . . . .
(founding member)
We support:
. . . . in the wild.

MEMBERSHIP CARD

The. . . . . .Club
Name:. . . . .
(founding member)
We support:
. . . . in the wild.

MEMBERSHIP CARD

The. . . . . .Club
Name:. . . . .
(founding member)
We support:
. . . . in the wild.

MEMBERSHIP CARD

The. . . . . .Club
Name:. . . . .
(founding member)
We support:
. . . . in the wild.

CLUB MEMBERSHIP CARD

CLUB MEMBERSHIP CARD

CLUB MEMBERSHIP CARD

CLUB MEMBERSHIP CARD

CLUB MEMBERSHIP CARD

CLUB MEMBERSHIP CARD

CLUB MEMBERSHIP CARD

CLUB MEMBERSHIP CARD

ANIMAL CAMOUFLAGE

Lots of animals use a disguise called 'camouflage' to keep safe. Some pretend that they are leaves and twigs, others change the colour of their skin to match their surroundings. Read the clues below, then guess which type of animal is hiding in each of the four pictures. Answers on page 60 to 61.

Seeing Stripes

Lions can only see in black and white, so to them these stripy creatures look just like wavy grass. What type of animal is hiding here and can you find four of them?

Sticky Situation

This twig-like insect can spend the whole day just sitting on a branch without anyone noticing. What type of insect could it be? Can you see it?

Colour Blind

This clever reptile changes the colour of its skin to match the trees and bushes where it lives. Do you know its name? Where is it hiding?

Sea Me

This eight-armed sea creature becomes almost invisible by changing the colour of its skin to blend into the sea bed. Which animal is it and can you spot it?

HOROSCOPE HEAVEN

Would you love to work with animals one day, but you're not sure which job is the one for you? Help is at hand with your *I Love Animals* horoscope. Whether you're destined to be a dog trainer or poised to be a pet psychologist, Horoscope Heaven will make you paws for thought and give you some great ideas for family days out.

Aries (21st March – 20th April)

You're so kind and caring that becoming an animal sanctuary owner is the perfect pathway for you. Visit a local pet sanctuary for a taste of this rewarding job.

Lucky animal: Sheep

Perfect colour match: Bright Orange

Cancer (22nd June – 23rd July)

You're most at home near the ocean, so how about making a splash as a dolphin trainer? Take a family trip to a water park and watch dolphins in action.

Lucky crustacean: Red Crab

Perfect colour match: Turquoise

Taurus (21st April – 21st May)

Nurturing and hard working – you'd be perfectly at home down on the farm. Many farms open their doors to the public, so you can pop along for a peek at farm life.

Lucky lizard: Chameleon

Perfect colour match: Lemon Yellow

Leo (24th July – 23rd August)

As a fiery Leo the lion, use your big cat passion to get a zoo keeping job. An outing to your local zoo provides a great opportunity to see zoo keepers at work.

Lucky lizard: Gecko

Perfect colour match: Scarlet

Gemini (22nd May – 21st June)

A job as a dog walker would suit your bouncy, energetic personality. Lots of dog homes are desperate for volunteer dog walkers – go and sniff them out.

Lucky bird: Pigeon

Perfect colour match: Sky Blue

Virgo (24th August – 23rd September)

You're always on hand to help with friends' problems, so why not become an animal psychologist? Follow the horse-taming instructions on page 19 for practice.

Lucky animal: Giraffe

Perfect colour match: Bottle Green

Libra (24th September – 23rd October)

In tune with your sensitive side and calm in a crisis, put your love of animals to life-saving use as a vet. At a hedgehog hospital you can see vets making a real difference.

Lucky bird: Puffin

Perfect colour match: Indigo

Capricorn (22nd December – 20th January)

You love getting your hands dirty, so how about being a conservation officer? Voluntary conservation work is a wonderful way to help the wildlife in your area.

Lucky animal: Otter

Perfect colour match: Pale Pink

Scorpio (24th October – 22nd November)

Your courageous nature would make you an excellent mounted police officer. Why not visit your local stables for a riding lesson, or offer to help out in the holidays.

Lucky crustacean: Lobster

Perfect colour match: Electric Blue

Aquarius (21st January – 19th February)

You always speak your mind, so you'd make a great campaigner for an animal charity. Why not become a member of a large animal organisation that you admire?

Lucky bird: Duck

Perfect colour match: Maroon

Sagittarius (23rd November – 21st December)

You're patient and great at getting results, so why not consider a career in dog-training. Visit a local dog show for tips, or better still ask to sit in on a real dog training class.

Lucky animal: Wild Pony

Perfect colour match: Dappled Grey

Pisces (20th February – 20th March)

You love all things scientific and are in awe of sea creatures, so why not be a marine biologist? Take a trip to your local aquarium for a head start.

Lucky fish: Trout

Perfect colour match: Bright Purple

ANIMAL ANTICS:
THREE COOL CARD GAMES

Animals really can give you hours and hours of fun. Just cut out the cards on pages 27 and 29, then choose one of these great games to play.

Memory Mayhem

Memory Mayhem is a mind-blowing game for two or more players.

1. Place one card of each animal on a tray, picture side up. (There are 18 different animals.)

2. Let the other players have a good look at the tray and try to remember all the cards.

3. Cover the cards with a tea-towel, so the players can't see what you're doing, and take one of the cards away.

4. Take off the cloth and show the tray to the players. Each player has to scribble down the animal card which they think is missing. Meanwhile, you write down which card you've taken away.

5. Keep doing this until you've removed all the cards. Now compare lists – the person with the most animals in the correct order wins.

Wild Animal Snap

1. Find one or more people to play with, then shuffle the cards and deal them out equally to all the players.

2. Everyone should hold their cards with the pattern side up. That way, they won't be able to see which card is next.

3. The player to the left of the dealer starts the game by putting down a card with the picture facing upwards. Carry on playing in a clockwise direction, keeping an eye out for two cards that look the same. When two matching cards are put down in a row quickly shout 'Snap!' and put your hand over the pile to claim the cards.

4. If a player loses all of their cards, they are out of the game. The winner is the player who spots the most 'Snaps' and ends up with all the cards.

Picking Pairs

You can play this game by yourself, or with friends.

1. Shuffle the cards so that they are really mixed up. Then lay them out in front of you in four rows of nine, pattern-side up.

2. Take it in turns to turn over two cards. If the cards are different animals study them carefully, then turn them face down again. If you find two with matching animals you keep the cards.

3. The trick with this game is to try to remember which animal cards you have seen and where they are. That way you'll be able to find a matching pair.

4. The person who finds the most pairs wins.

TOP TIPS FOR SPOTTING WILD ANIMALS

In the country, people are used to seeing wildlife all around them. But even in towns and cities it's amazing how many wild animals you can spot if you just know how to look or listen for them.

Bird Detective

The morning is the best time to spot our feathered friends. So, when you hear a dawn chorus, stand outside and tune your ears to a particular bird's song or call. Spend a few moments working out which direction the sound is coming from, then slowly walk towards it. Take small steps and tread softly – you don't want to scare the bird away.

When the call sounds much clearer, look above you – the bird should be perched in a tree, or resting in another high place.

Use a bird handbook to work out which type of bird you've found and before long you'll recognise its song.

Why not put a bird box in your garden or hang a bird feeder near a window – that way you'll get to see some birds really close up!

Night Watch

At night try watching from a window for movements in the shadows. Remember to turn off the indoor light as you peek outside, or you might scare away your nocturnal pals.

Hedgehogs, foxes and badgers are most adventurous at night, so why not leave them out a bowl of tinned cat or dog food. Only put out a small amount of food, or the animals may become too dependent on it and stop hunting for food themselves.

You'll find hedgehogs are really hungry in Autumn because they need to fatten up for a deep Winter sleep, called 'hibernation'.

Female hedgehogs will be especially grateful for food in Spring and Summer, when they are feeding their young.

Frogtastic

On a family day out, stop off at a pond and look for signs of frogs – their life cycle is fascinating and they grow from an egg into an adult in just 12 to 16 weeks.

If it's Spring, look for a mass of see-through jelly just below the surface of the water, called 'frogspawn'. The dark spots inside the jelly are the frog's eggs.

If you visit the pond a few weeks later, you'll see small, dark 'tadpoles' swimming around – these have hatched from the jelly eggs. For a closer look, use a dipper net to catch a few. Place them in a bucket with some pond water, before returning them safely to the pond.

Over the next few weeks the tadpoles will develop front and back legs. Their bodies will get longer as they grow into baby frogs called 'froglets'. When they have lost their tails and become adults, the frogs will climb out of the pond and onto dry land.

IN A TIGHT SPOT

It's best to avoid dangerous animals, but if you ever found yourself caught in a tricky situation would you know what to do? Don't try this at home!

Shark Shock

Shark attacks are very rare, and there are lots of things you can do to avoid them. It's best not to swim in places where sharks are known to live. Also, don't go swimming alone, and don't swim far from the shore.

If you do see a shark, stay still to avoid attracting its attention. If it approaches you, leave the water quickly, but calmly.

Should the shark attack, don't play dead – fight back! Hit the shark in the eye as hard as you can and hopefully it will swim away.

Alligator Attack

Don't go paddling in an area where alligators swim. If you do see an alligator, keep a safe distance from it. Do not throw things at the animal or feed it.

If you see some alligator babies, do not try to play with them – they are not cute and you can bet there will be a protective adult lurking near by.

If an alligator does bite you, put up a struggle and create lots of noise to confuse it. Make your escape by running in a straight line – alligators can outswim a human all day, but they can only run for about 10 metres before tiring themselves out.

Bear Cheek

If a bear comes into your camp site it's probably just hungry. Even so, try to avoid attracting a bear in the first place. Don't keep food in your tent. Put it inside a plastic bag and hang it from the high branch of a tree, at least 4 metres in the air and out of reach of the trunk. The tree should be a safe distance from your camp site, too.

If you do see a bear, do not run away and do not climb a tree. Talk to the bear and hold your hands high above your head so you look bigger than you are. Keep talking to it as you slowly back away.

Rhino Rumpus

Most rhinos are timid animals and will not attack you if you leave them alone. They can, however, be extremely dangerous when angry.

Female rhinos are fiercely protective of their babies, so treat them with extra caution. If Mum snorts at you, take it as a warning – if you don't leave soon, she could charge.

If a rhino does charge angrily towards you, quickly climb a nearby tree. Rhinos have terrible eyesight, so hopefully the rhino will not see you in the tree and will keep on running.

JUNGLE FUN

You've won a dream holiday to the jungle where you meet a brother and sister, Jack and Jenny. From trekking and tracking to rucksack packing, these puzzles will take you on a jungle adventure that you won't forget. Turn to page 61 for all the answers.

1. ANIMAL ANSWERS

Your first day in the jungle will be full of amazing sights that you never normally see. Use the clues below to guess the six different animals you might spot.

Which jungle creature. . .

1. . . .has bad eyesight, no legs and sheds its skin?
2. . . .is brightly coloured and can speak, if taught?
3. . . .is stripy and has babies called 'cubs'?
4. . . .has eight legs, unlike insects, which have six legs?
5. . . .swims in rivers, but can also walk on land, and has big, powerful jaws?
6. . . .hangs upside down in trees and loves to sleep?

2. WHO'S EATING WHO?

All the animals in the jungle have to eat to survive, but which animal eats which food? Can you match the animals below with the food they often eat?

Animal	Food
Deer	Fruit and leaves
Jaguar	Grubs
Toucan	Leaves
Gibbon	Deer
Iguana	Fruit and insects

3. SPOT THE DIFFERENCE

Jack is getting ready to set out and explore the jungle. Before he goes, Jack needs to check that he has everything for the trip. Can you spot what's missing from his jungle gear in the second picture? There are six differences to find.

4. DOT-TO-DOT

Jenny can't wait to find out what surprises the jungle has in store for her. She's carefully packed her rucksack with everything she'll need for the day. But who's that stealing her snacks? Join up the dots to reveal a cheeky friend.

5. JUNGLE JAM

On the way back to the campsite you surprise four jungle friends. Can you put these tree-top creatures in their correct places? Every row, column and mini-grid of four squares must contain one of each of these four animals:

TOP TRACKER

Tracking is a skill that is fun to learn. All you need to do is find some tracks and you can begin. All kinds of animals leave trails, even small ones such as insects, so you can practise tracking without going more than a few metres. If you are going further afield, family days out provide top tracking opportunities.

1. Great Shapes

Animals leave tracks in the snow during Winter and these tracks are often very easy to spot. In warmer weather, look for tracks in soil or sand. In dry areas, you can even find animal prints in the dust.

It's a good idea to know what sort of animal you're following. Use an animal track guide to identify the tracks of animals in your area. You may cross paths with wild animals, such as birds, rabbits or foxes, and with pets, such as dogs and cats.

Look closely at the shape of the tracks you are going to follow. Notice their size and shape, so that you can be sure you are following the same tracks further down the line. You might even like to measure the length of a print – the length of an animal's body, not including its neck or tail, is about ten times as long as its footprint.

It's fairly easy to work out which direction most animals are travelling in, as you'll be able to tell from the direction of their toe prints.

2. On The Right Track

While tracking an animal, don't forget to pay attention to where you are – it's easy to get caught up with the trail, especially in woods or forests. Keep an eye out for landmarks, or leave a trail made of pebbles.

If your tracking is successful, you may come face to face with the animal itself. Whatever kind of creature you find, treat it respectfully. Watch it from a safe distance, keep still so you don't frighten it and back away slowly.

3. Read The Signs

Look out for other signs of animal movement too, such as broken twigs or bent grass. This can help you follow the animal if you lose its tracks for a while. If this does happen, mark the last track with a stick, or other object, so that you can find it again easily, and look around the area until you find another print. Asking yourself where you would go, if you were the animal, can often point you in the right direction.

THE FOOTPRINT MAZE

Now you've learnt how to track animals in the wild, can you master The Footprint Maze? Follow this footprint 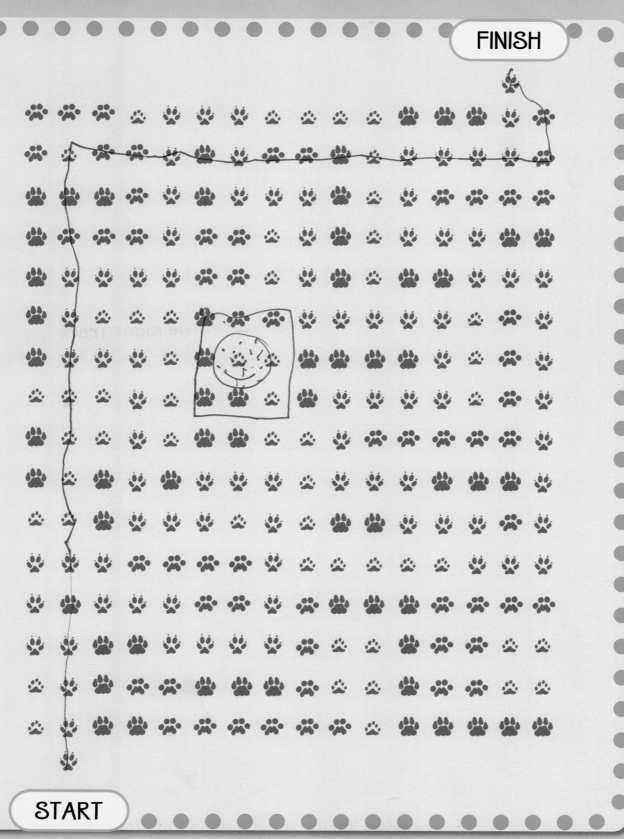 from the START to the FINISH. You can move in any direction, apart from diagonally. The correct path is on page 61.

FINISH

START

A fun pet that's easy to look after.

Which type of TV programme would you rather watch?

An underwater documentary about sea life.

WHICH ANIMAL SHOULD YOU ADOPT?

Lots of charities and zoos run schemes where you can adopt an animal. It's a great way of helping your favourite animals and you get an adoption certificate and pictures in return. Follow this flow-chart to figure out which wild animal is right for you...

A programme about big cats in Africa.

If you were choosing a pet, which would you prefer?

Maths – I enjoy a challenge and like working on my own.

Start

A cute pet that I can cuddle up to.

At school, which of these would be your favourite lesson?

Drama – I love working in a group and putting on a performance.

MIDNIGHT FEASTS

Some animals are nocturnal, which means they like to sleep during the day and get up when you're fast asleep. If you have a pet cat you might have noticed that it likes to nap during the day, when all you want to do is play. This is because cats go out to hunt at night. In the wild, animals get up to all sorts of interesting things at night. Just take a look at this lot...

The green tree frog can make itself darker, or lighter, if it needs to hide.

Hedgehog

They may not be able to see very well, but these spiky little animals have a great sense of smell and brilliant hearing. While you are sleeping, they snuffle about looking for insects, and sometimes even eat a mouse or a frog.

Green Tree Frog

This amphibian lives in warm areas in the southern states of America. In the day it sits in the shade by ponds and lakes, but at night it is wide awake, hopping about to find food such as cockroaches, spiders and flies.

At the end of the night, these bush babies cuddle up and spend the day sleeping in a leafy nest.

Bush Baby

Bush babies live in Africa and spend most of their time in trees. Luckily for them they have long tails to balance in the branches and huge eyes to help them see in the dark. Bush babies mainly eat insects such as caterpillars and dung beetles.

Badger

Badgers live in woodland tunnels called 'setts'. At night, they shuffle around looking for small animals to eat such as mice and rats, as well as insects. Badgers also like peanuts – but not the salted or dry-roasted kind.

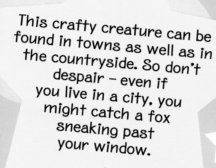

If you live in an area where badgers live, why not leave some unsalted peanuts scattered around for them to find?

This crafty creature can be found in towns as well as in the countryside. So don't despair – even if you live in a city, you might catch a fox sneaking past your window.

Fox

In the dark hours foxes hunt for insects, fruit, birds, eggs and small animals. They even steal chickens if they are not carefully penned away.

Owl

Owls are perfectly equipped to spot their prey in the dark. They have huge, silent wings, so they can hover in the air without making any noise, and can suddenly swoop down to grab a furry little animal such as a mouse, mole or rabbit. Owls can even swallow small animals whole.

FACT ATTACK

We may think humans are pretty great – and we are – but other animals are fascinating too. Just look at some of these incredible facts…

Big Deal
The biggest animal alive today is the blue whale. It can grow to a whopping 30 metres long and weigh 150 tonnes. That's about 20 times as heavy as an African elephant.

A Tall Order
The tallest bird is the ostrich, at over 2.5 metres. It's also the fastest running bird. It can keep running for several minutes at 50 kilometres per hour and in short bursts even reaches 70 kilometres per hour, which is about the same speed as a racehorse.

Great Leaps
Some poison arrow frogs are so tiny they are less than a centimetre in length. But the goliath frog can grow up to 32 centimetres long – that's even longer than this page.

What An Ape
Gorillas are the biggest apes, at about the same height as an adult human. They are vegetarian and only eat plants (apart from the odd insect they might accidentally munch, of course).

Dizzy Heights
The giraffe is the tallest land animal, standing at over 5 metres in height. Its neck alone is almost 2 metres long – about the same length as an adult man is tall.

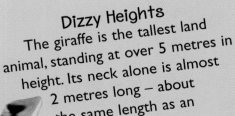

Not So Fast

The cheetah is the fastest land animal over short distances. This athletic cat can run at almost 100 kilometres per hour, whereas people can only reach about 36 kilometres per hour over 100 metres. Antelopes, like the one shown here, can run faster than a cheetah over long distances.

Go With The Flow

Reindeer are such good swimmers that they can cross wide, fast-flowing rivers. They also trek hundreds of kilometres every year just to find enough vegetation to eat.

Happy Birthday, Again

Elephants can live for up to 70 years. If it's true they never forget, that's a lot to remember! Orcas, also known as killer whales (shown below), can live for up to 90 years. But tortoises can beat even that – some live to celebrate their 120th birthday.

What A Howler

Dogs have lived alongside humans for thousands of years. Experts believe that dogs have descended from wolves – which can grow to about 2 metres in length, including their tails. It's hard to believe that today's tiny, 'toy' dog breeds are related to these wild creatures.

TOP FIVE ANIMALS

We can't help having our favourites when it comes to the animal kingdom. But what about those animals we love for their more quirky qualities?

TOP FIVE
Laziest Animals

Hippopotamus
A hippo spends most of the day bathing in water or wallowing in mud. It even produces a red sweat that acts as sunscreen.

Koala
This nocturnal animal spends up to 19 hours a day sleeping and 3 hours eating.

Sloth
The sloth sleeps in the trees for 15 hours a day and visits the ground only once a week, for a wee.

Giant Tortoise
Found on the Galapagos Islands, these super-slow movers spend most of the day lazing in the sun and grazing on plants.

Domestic Cat
Pet cats have an amazing ability to fall asleep almost instantly. This is where we get the name 'cat nap' from.

TOP FIVE
Noisiest Animals

Blue Whale
Thought to be the loudest animal in the world, the blue whale can make deep rumbling sounds that are louder than a plane taking off.

Cicada
This is the loudest insect in the world. It calls out if it's in danger and sings to attract females.

Howler Monkey
The howler monkey is the loudest monkey and the loudest animal on land. This animal's loud whooping can be heard up to 4.8 kilometres away.

Kittiwake
This elegant seagull is so noisy that it is named after the sound of its call: 'kittee-wa-aaake'.

Barn Owl
The beautiful barn owl may look like a peaceful bird, but if you heard its shrill screeches at night, you might jump out of your skin.

TOP FIVE
Strangest Pets

Tarantula
Big, hairy, but doesn't need a lot of looking after – the tarantula makes an interesting pet. But watch out, it can bite!

Wallaby
This miniature kangaroo makes a playful pal, but requires a lot of care – baby wallabies must be fed from a bottle several times a day.

Skunk
A skunk sprays a seriously pongy liquid when it feels threatened. If you don't watch out, it might steal your clothes to make a snuggly bed.

Potbellied Pig
Sociable and intelligent, the potbellied pig loves to have its tummy scratched, and can be trained to walk on a lead.

Stick Insect
Long, thin and well-camouflaged, pet stick insects need fresh food and a spray of water every day.

TOP FIVE
Greediest Animals

Larva Of The Polyphemus Moth
This caterpillar eats 86,000 times its own weight in tree leaves during the first two months of its life.

Lion
The king of the jungle can kill and eat a wide variety of large mammals. Lions will even eat a baby elephant if they are hungry enough.

Wolverine
Wolverine means 'greedy'. This animal will eat anything from birds' eggs to deer. It sprays its prey with scent to stop other animals eating it.

Tiger Shark
This ferocious predator eats almost anything it can catch. It has even been known to eat other sharks and swallow car number plates.

Mosquito
The mosquito sucks the blood of mammals – injecting them with a chemical that makes it easier to suck out more blood.

MAN OR MONKEY?

Most humans you meet aren't as hairy as other apes, but we are part of the ape family, along with gorillas, orangutans, chimpanzees and gibbons. Monkeys are part of a different, but similar group of mammals. All of us are 'primates' – a group of mammals that have certain features in common such as two arms and two legs, instead of four legs.

A Swinging Time

Most apes have forward-facing eyes that are good for working out distance. They have well-developed brains, making them almost as intelligent as humans. Flexible arms help them swing from branch to branch and they do not have tails. Monkeys have less flexible shoulders and arms than apes, and prefer to run along branches using their tails to balance, rather than swinging from them.

A Gripping Tail

Many monkeys, such as tamarins and marmosets, have tails which are 'prehensile'. This means they can use their tails to grip branches and other objects.

Most macaques do not have tails even though they are monkeys, not apes. Macaques are the most widespread primates after humans. They live in lots of different types of habitat, in places such as Africa and Japan.

People are very similar to apes – just look at the human-like way this orangutan holds its hands.

Not Just A Pretty Face

Monkeys and apes are what we call 'intelligent' animals. Intelligent animals can communicate, have good memories and are able to solve problems.

Human Interest

If you visit a wildlife park or watch gorillas on television, you'll be amazed at how like us they seem. In fact, when looking into a gorilla's eyes many people feel that the animal is looking back, as interested in us as we are in them.

The macaque monkey has many different homes – from the tropical forests of India, to the mountains of Morocco.

CHIMPS AND CREEPERS

Help! You're stuck on the jungle floor and there's a crazy crocodile on the loose. Chimps and Creepers is a game for 2 to 4 players. The aim of the game (see page 49) is to escape to safety by reaching the bunch of bananas as quickly as possible. There are friendly chimpanzees to give you a helping hand, but try to avoid the slippery creepers or you'll fall back down again!

1.
Cut out the counters and spinner below. Put the middle of the spinner over a piece of sticky putty or a squashy eraser and push a hole through it with the point of a pencil. Take away the putty or eraser, and work the pencil through the spinner so that about 3 centimetres of it is poking through.

2.
To begin the game, each player takes a turn to spin the spinner. The player who spins the highest number begins the game by moving the number of spaces shown on the side of the spinner that touches the table. You might want to paste a cardboard backing to the spinner to make it sturdier.

3.
Each player then takes it in turn to spin the spinner and then move forward that number of squares. If you land on a square with a creeper hanging down from it, you must slide down to where it ends. If you land on a square with a chimpanzee's hand in it, jump up to join the cheeky chimp in his square. The winner is the first player to reach the bananas.

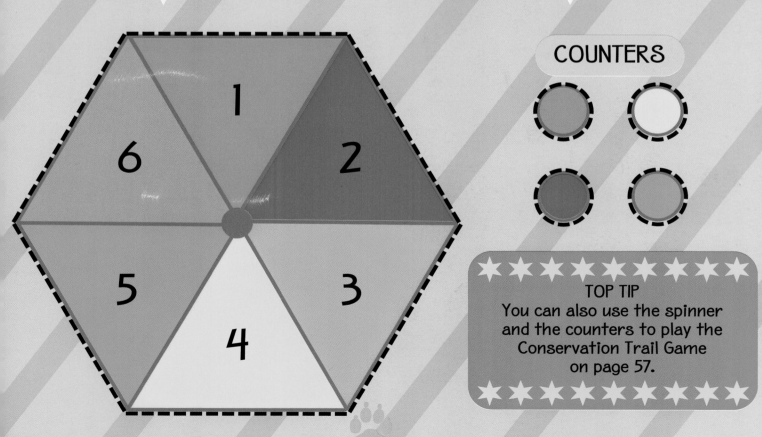

COUNTERS

TOP TIP
You can also use the spinner and the counters to play the Conservation Trail Game on page 57.

CHIMPS AND CREEPERS BOARD

Cut out the spinner and counters on page 47. Then follow the Chimps And Creepers instructions to move back and forth across the board, in the direction of the arrows. First to the bananas wins!

GOING, GOING, GONE?

All of the animals on this page have been rated 'critically endangered'.
This means there is a very high chance they will die out in the
immediate future. They need our help urgently.

Why Are Some Animals Dying Out?

Some animals suffer because their homes are
disappearing, for example when rainforests are cut
down or wetlands are drained for farmland. Even
though the law protects them, other animals are
hunted for their fur, their tusks, or to be sold
as pets.

Zoo Time

People in zoos are working hard to make sure that
animals in danger will survive. Whenever possible,
conservation programmes protect animals in zoos
until their numbers increase and they can be
returned to the wild.

Leatherback Turtle

There are many different species of turtle and many of them are in danger
of dying out. The leatherback turtle is the largest of all and is critically
endangered. People thought the Arakan forest turtle from Myanmar
(Burma) had already died out. However, it is very rare and it is possible
that just a few are left living in the wild.

Tigers

Tigers are hunted for their skins, and many body parts of tigers are still
used in Chinese medicines. Tigers were once found all over Asia and
south-east Asia, but now three kinds of tiger are already extinct and
three more are critically endangered. It's estimated that there are fewer
than 50 south China tigers left in the wild.

Giant Ibis

Experts guess that there are fewer than 50 giant ibis left in the
wild. Many of the wetlands where the giant ibis spends its time are
being turned into farmland. In Cambodia and Laos, where the birds live,
the government is trying to make people understand how rare these
birds are. Hopefully everyone will start to look after the ones that are
left. The giant ibis is a huge bird, which grows to over a metre in length.

Rhinoceros

Of the five species of rhinoceros that are left, the black rhino, Javan
rhino and the Sumatran rhino are critically endangered. Javan rhinos live
in Indonesia and Vietnam, but there are possibly as few as 60 left in the
wild. The number of Indian rhinos left in the wild went down to fewer
than 200 at one time, but they are now well protected and numbers
have risen to about 2,500.

Iberian Lynx

The Iberian lynx lives in only two small areas of Spain. It is the most endangered cat in the world, and there are only about 100 left in the wild. Human beings hunt the Iberian lynx for its fur. Humans are the animals' only predator.

Red Wolf

The red wolf is only found in a small area of North Carolina in the USA, and there are fewer than 150 left in the wild. With such a small population, even bad weather can threaten the survival of these wolves, but the main threat to them is still being hunted by humans.

Orange-Bellied Parrot

The orange-bellied parrot lives in Tasmania, Australia. In the last hundred years their numbers have dropped dramatically, and now there are fewer than 200 left in the wild.

Asiatic Lion

This lion lives in just one forest in India and is threatened by disease, natural disasters and the local people who hunt it. The Asiatic lion is slightly smaller than the African lion and has a less noticeable mane.

Mountain Gorillas

There are only a few hundred mountain gorillas left in the world. Civil war, poaching, disease and forest clearance have made life very difficult for them. The forests where they live span areas of Rwanda, Uganda and the Democratic Republic of Congo. Conservation projects have increased their numbers, but they still need a lot of help.

Sumatran Orangutans

There are fewer than 7,500 Sumatran orangutans living in the wild. Hundreds of orangutans are disappearing every year and their only predators are people. Orangutans spend most of their time in the trees, but the rainforest in Indonesia is quickly disappearing. Orangutan originally meant 'Person of the Forest' and these clever creatures are one of our closest relatives in the ape world.

ORIGAMI ANIMALS

ORIGAMI CRANE

This crazy crane might look a bit tricky to make, but it's well worth the effort. The Japanese believe that if you have a special wish, you should make 1,000 cranes. By the time you've finished making them, your wish will have been granted.

Start with a square piece of paper.

1. Make two diagonal folds – by folding A to D and B to C. Turn it over and fold the bottom half of the square across the middle to make a crease, and the left side of the square over the right side to make another crease.

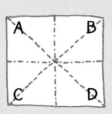

2. Gently press all four corners together and flatten your square along the folded lines.

You should now have a smaller square.

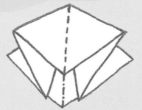

3. Hold the square by the bottom point and fold the two lower sides into the centre. Press firmly.

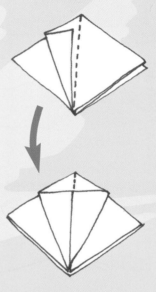

4. Now take the top point of the square and fold it over the top as shown. Press firmly.

5. These are your crease lines. Open the crease lines out flat again.

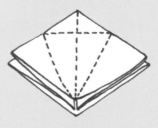

6. Lift up the top layer of the square from the lower corner so that it opens out like a flower.

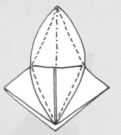

7. Fold the paper back along the crease lines you made, pulling the paper out into a long diamond shape.

8. Repeat steps 3 to 7 on the other side. This is your bird base.

9. Now fold the two lower sides into the centre and press firmly.

10. Repeat step 9 on the other side so that you have a narrow kite shape.

11. Fold the right-hand point up and to the side. Make a firm crease. This will be the neck and head of your bird.

12. Now you need to reverse the fold so that the neck comes out from the middle. Do this by opening the point out a little, then refolding the neck on the inside, along the crease lines you just made.

13. Now repeat steps 11 to 12 with the other point. This is your bird's tail.

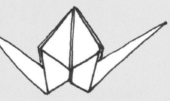

14. For the head, make a fold in the neck pointing downwards. Then reverse the fold again as in step 12.

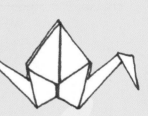

15. Now your origami should really start to look like a bird. Pull each of the large flaps down gently so that the wings point to the side.

16. If you pull them apart slowly, the back of the bird should open into a square. Push the back in slightly and your crane is complete!

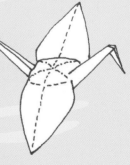

WHAT ELSE CAN I DO?

Are you angry about animal exploitation? Are you terrified that some types of tiger are dying out? Are you gobsmacked by the effects of global warming?
Don't panic!
There are lots of things you can do to help animals around the world and protect the environments in which they live. It doesn't matter how small your action is, everything helps and saving animals is fun.

GET PLANTING

Plants are one of the first stages in the 'food chain' – animals eat plants and then those animals are eaten by other animals, and so on.

• Grow some insect-friendly flowers in your garden (these are available from nurseries and seed suppliers). This will attract bugs and butterflies which will, in turn, attract birds and small animals, such as hedgehogs, to your garden.

• Talk to your parents or local farmers about how important a hedge is as a home to many different kinds of wildlife. It should be looked after, not chopped down.

• If you live in a city, find out about local tree-planting projects that you could get involved with. Better still, start one yourself.

DON'T BE RUBBISH

Here are two really simple things you can do:

• Every year over a million sea creatures are killed by plastic bags that end up in the water. On land, animals can eat plastic bags mistaking them for food, and this can cause them fatal damage. Buy your household a reusable shopping bag. Make sure anyone who goes shopping takes it and avoids using plastic bags.

• Animals and birds die from being trapped in or strangled by six-pack holders and cans. When you buy canned drinks, cut up the plastic holders that keep the cans together. When you have finished your drink, crush the empty can with the metal ring-pull inside it.

PET RESCUE

Charities and campaigns all over the world need your help to save pets from cruel treatment and from being abandoned.

• You could raise money to donate to a charity or offer them your time to help out.

• If you want to get a pet, why not go to an animal rescue centre and adopt an abandoned animal that really needs your love.

GO ONLINE

It's important to spread the word. Tell everyone you know what you are doing to save animals and the environment. Encourage them to do the same.

• Use the Internet to research projects and charities in your area that are helping local wildlife.

• If you have your own web page, why not add some information about what people can do to help animals?

• Check out the World Wildlife Fund website at www.worldwildlife.org
The WWF is saving wildlife, protecting habitats, and addressing global threats. Four million people around the world are busy protecting animals. Find out what you can do to make a difference.

A TEMPLATE LETTER

Here is an example of a letter that you could send to your local council, to ask about how they are caring for the wildlife in your area and the environment. You can change the letter according to the type of organisation you are writing to.

THE COUNCILLOR'S NAME
THE COUNCIL'S ADDRESS

YOUR ADDRESS
THE DATE

Dear Mr/Mrs . . . . ,

As a young resident of (your nearest town or city), I am keen to find out how the council is tackling environmental issues and protecting local wildlife.

Please can you tell me more about your current wildlife and environmental campaigns, as well as those campaigns you hope to start in the future.

I would also like to find out about any wildlife or environmental campaigns that I could contribute to in my area.

Yours sincerely,

YOUR NAME

If you know the name of the person you are writing to, use it with their job title on the envelope and letter. Finish your letter with 'Yours sincerely'. If you don't know their name, address your envelope using their job title, and write 'Dear Sir/Madam in your letter. Finish it with 'Yours faithfully'.

CONSERVATION TRAIL GAME

Use the counters and spinner on page 47 and make your way around the islands to rescue four baby animals. Start on stepping stone 1 and stay alert in case you land on one of the red steps listed below. First to the Conservation Champion Trophy wins.

Step 1: START HERE

Step 6: You must spin a 6 to get to the island and rescue the panda.

Step 11: The panda is hungry – go back 2 steps.

Step 13: Trapped in a swamp – miss a turn.

Step 14: You must spin a 6 to get to the island and rescue the rhino.

Step 19: The rhino's in a rush – skip ahead 4 steps.

Step 23: You must spin a 6 to get to the island and rescue the gorilla.

Step 28: The gorilla wants to play – go back 3 steps.

Step 32: You are attacked by crocodiles – miss a turn.

Step 34: You must spin a 6 to get to the island and rescue the tiger.

Step 36: You are stuck in a storm – miss a turn.

Step 41: You must spin a 6 to become Conservation Champion!

THE FINAL CHALLENGE QUIZ

Now you've read this book — test your knowledge with our final challenge quiz. The answers are on page 61. Pencils at the ready!

1. Which bird cannot fly but runs at top speeds?

A. Flamingo
B. Canary
C. Ostrich
D. Penguin

2. If you were trying to make friends with a horse, which of these should you not do?

A. Gently stroke its neck
B. Make lots of loud noises
C. Walk up to it from the side so that it can see you
D. Offer it a carrot

3. Which of these is the odd one out and do you know why?

A. Fox
B. Hedgehog
C. Worm
D. Badger

4. When you are camping in bear country, where should you keep your food?

A. On the top of a car
B. Inside your tent
C. Safe beside you
D. Hanging from the branch of a tree

5. What should you do if a shark starts swimming towards you?

A. Call it lots of names
B. Scream at it loudly
C. Leave the water quickly, but calmly
D. Thrash around in the water

6.

Which of these animals sweats a red sunscreen?

A. Potbellied pig
B. Rhino
C. Giraffe
D. Hippo

9.

Which of these birds is critically endangered?

A. Parrot
B. Peregrine falcon
C. Giant ibis
D. Owl

7.

What do pandas spend most of their lives eating?

A. Insects
B. Bamboo
C. Small rodents
D. Cake

10.

Which of the facts below is untrue?

A. The largest animal on land is the African bush elephant
B. Male seahorses give birth to their young
C. Pet dogs are distantly related to wolves
D. An elephant can walk at speeds of over 50 kilometres per hour

8.

What is the name of the loudest monkey in the world?

A. The macaque
B. The howler monkey
C. The baboon
D. The orangutan

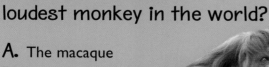

ALL THE ANSWERS

Page 10 – What Kind Of Animal Are You?

MOSTLY As: An Excellent Elephant
You are very thoughtful and you always remember your friends' birthdays, but if anyone steps on your toes, you get angry.

MOSTLY Bs: A Wandering Wolf
You are playful, have lots of energy, and love the company of others. You might whine if you're away from friends for too long.

MOSTLY Cs: An Honourable Owl
You are extremely clever and very good at making decisions. You enjoy nothing better than staying up late with a good book.

MOSTLY Ds: A Mischievous Mongoose
You make friends easily, but can be a little nervous. You are great at keeping an eye out for any approaching danger.

MOSTLY Es: A Champion Cheetah
You are very resourceful and always like to be the winner. You sometimes hiss a little bit when you get angry.

Page 18 – True Or False?

1. **False:** There are three species of zebra and each species has a different number of stripes.
2. **True:** Flamingos turn their heads upside down so they can strain the water out of their food, because they mostly eat shrimp and algae.
3. **True:** The Cuban bee hummingbird weighs just 2 grams, which is less than two paper clips.
4. **False:** An elephant can reach speeds of over 24 kilometres per hour, but because all its feet are never off the ground at the same time it is actually just walking very quickly.
5. **False:** A hippopotamus can run faster than a human.
6. **True:** A giraffe can clean its ears with its tongue.
7. **False:** A butterfly has thousands of eyes.
8. **True:** This is because the crocodile's tongue is attached to the base of its mouth.
9. **False:** Dolphins sleep with one eye open. This is because only half of their brain can go to sleep at any one time.
10. **True:** This is so that the camel can protect its eyes from blowing sand.
11. **True:** An ostrich's brain is the size of its eyeball.
12. **True:** A female seahorse lays its eggs in a pouch that a male seahorse has on its stomach.

Page 23 – Animal Camouflage

Four zebras

A stick insect

A chameleon

Page 34 – Jungle Fun

Animal Answers

1. Snake
2. Parrot
3. Tiger
4. Spider
5. Crocodile
6. Sloth

Who's Eating Who?

Deer eat leaves.
Jaguars eat deer.
Toucans eat fruit and insects.
Gibbons eat fruit and leaves.
Iguanas eat grubs.

Spot The Difference

1. Jack's hatband is missing.
2. His watch has gone.
3. The map is blank.
4. Jack's pocket has vanished.
5. He has lost a sock.
6. There is a strap missing on Jack's rucksack.

Dot-to-Dot

It's a cheeky chimpanzee.

An eight-legged octopus

Jungle Jam

Page 37 – The Footprint Maze

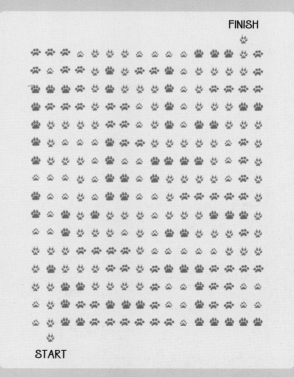

Page 58 – The Final Challenge Quiz

1. **C**   2. **B**   3. **C** (Worm – all the others are mammals).   4. **D**   5. **C**
6. **D**   7. **B**   8. **B**   9. **C**   10. **D**